ON THE HUNT WITH
OWLS

SANDRA MARKLE

Lerner Publications ◆ Minneapolis

THE ANIMAL WORLD IS FULL OF PREDATORS.

Predators are the hunters that find, catch, and eat other animals—their prey—in order to survive. Every environment has its chain of hunters. The smaller, slower, less able predators become part of the prey for the bigger, faster, more cunning hunters. But everywhere, just a few kinds of predators are at the top of the food chain. These are the top predators. In nearly every habitat of the world, except Antarctica, this group includes one or more kinds of owls. Scientists currently list about 260 different kinds of owls. Two of the largest are the Eurasian eagle owl and the great gray owl. Eurasian eagle owls are found in woodlands, grasslands, deserts, and mountainous areas throughout Europe, Asia, and northern Africa. Great gray owls live in forests in North America, Scandinavia, Russia, and Mongolia.

GREAT GRAY OWL

EURASIAN EAGLE OWL

3

EURASIAN
EAGLE OWL

4

Why are Eurasian eagle owls and great gray owls top predators? For one thing, the adults are big. Eagle owls may take prey as big as martens. Great gray owls may kill rabbits.

Females are even bigger than the males, but they're still light enough to fly. An adult female Eurasian eagle owl has a body about 30 inches (75 cm) long with a 6-foot-2 (188 cm) wingspan but only weighs about 5.9 pounds (2.7 kg). An adult female great gray owl has a body about 33 inches (84 cm) long with a 5-foot (152 cm) wingspan but weighs about 2.8 pounds (1.3 kg).

WOW!
A great gray owl has the longest tail of any type of owl.

Another reason these owls are top predators is because they fly *very* quietly. That's perfect for surprising prey! These hunters are so stealthy because the edges of their wing feathers are fringed. Air rushing over the wing feathers of other kinds of birds during flight stirs air currents, which makes sounds. The fringed edges of an owl's wing feathers don't stir air currents.

GREAT GRAY OWL

8

These owls are also top predators because they're armed with powerful weapons: large talon-tipped toes and a sharp beak. Like all owls, each of these owls grabs its prey with its feet. It turns the outer toe on each foot to have two of its toes point forward and two point backward. That gives it a crushing grip as it digs its sharp talons into the prey. If that's not enough, the owl finishes the kill with a bite of its sharp beak.

Since no owl can chew, this predator's digestive system must do all the work. First, what it swallows goes into a stomachlike part. There, strong digestive juices begin to break down the food. Next, the food passes into a muscular sac called the gizzard. This helps grind up the food into a soft mass that's passed on to the intestine to finish digestion. But the gizzard also blocks and holds any bit not broken down, such as teeth, bones, and fur. The gizzard packs those bits into a waste pellet. Within a few more hours, the owl brings up the waste pellet. Then it lowers its head, opens its beak wide, and lets the pellet drop out of its mouth.

OWL PELLET

WOW!
New feathers grow out of the bird's skin the way hairs do on other animals.

Between flights, Eurasian eagle owls and great gray owls do what all owls do—preen. To do that, an owl gently pulls its feathers—one at a time—through its beak. Feathers are made up of hundreds of strands held together by tiny hooks. Flying can cause these to unhook. Preening fastens the feather strands together again.

But flying is still hard on feathers. So owls regularly molt, or shed old feathers and grow new ones. Wing and tail flight feathers are replaced each year—but just a few at a time. Wing flight feathers are shed and replaced from the right and left wings at the same time and in the same order. That way, the bird stays balanced in flight.

WOW!
Great gray owls have the largest facial disks of any owl.

14

Another reason Eurasian eagle owls and great gray owls are top predators is their keen hearing. All owls hear sounds ten times fainter than humans can detect. That lets eagle owls and great grays hear prey when it's too dark to see well. Such good hearing happens partly because an owl's facial feathers create disks that scoop up and focus sounds to its ear openings. Those are under the outer edge of its facial disk. One ear opening is also a little higher on the owl's head than the other one. That difference helps the owl judge the direction a sound came from so it can home in on prey.

To home in on exactly where a sound is coming from, the owl turns its head. An owl can turn its head about 270 degrees, which is much farther than a human head turns. An owl can turn its head that far because its neck has fourteen neck bones—twice as many as the human neck.

EURASIAN EAGLE OWL

EURASIAN EAGLE OWL

NICTITATING
MEMBRANE

Like all owls, Eurasian eagle owls and great gray owls can see very well. Their eyes are big and have powerful magnifying lenses to spot small prey across long distances. An owl's pupils—what look like dark eyespots—open extra wide to let light enter its eyes and strike the retina. This special layer at the back of each eye is covered with light-sensitive cells that send signals to the brain. Once its brain interprets these signals, an owl *sees*.

But an owl's eyes also have a mirrorlike layer behind the retina. This layer bounces light that passed through the retina back through it again. More light is gathered for better vision in dim light.

To protect its big eyes, an owl has three eyelids. The third eyelid, called the nictitating membrane, cleans the owl's eyes and acts like goggles during flight.

Another key reason Eurasian eagle owls and great gray owls are top predators is that they learn how to hunt from other top predators—their parents. A male great gray owl claims a territory and calls to attract a mate. Each year he is likely to pair with a different female. When a female joins him, the male courts her by catching and bringing her many food gifts. This proves his hunting ability in his territory. When she eats these gifts, she accepts being his mate. Then the pair finds a nest site.

Eurasian eagle owls mate in late January or early February. They start early because their young need to master hunting during the summer when prey is plentiful. An eagle owl pair doesn't build a nest. Instead, they choose a nest site: a rock ledge, a crevice on a cliff, or even a place on the ground.

After mating, the female deposits as many as four eggs. The male brings food while she incubates the eggs with her body heat. After about a month, the owlets hatch. At first, their eyes are shut tight and they only have a thin down coat. They need their mother's warmth and to be fed often. The father continues to deliver prey, and the mother tears off small bits to feed each owlet.

When the owlets are about four days old, their eyes open. And they have a thicker down coat. As they keep growing, they become stronger—and hungrier.

WOW!
While incubating the eggs, a female owl only leaves the nest and the eggs exposed for a few minutes at a time to pass wastes.

EURASIAN EAGLE OWL

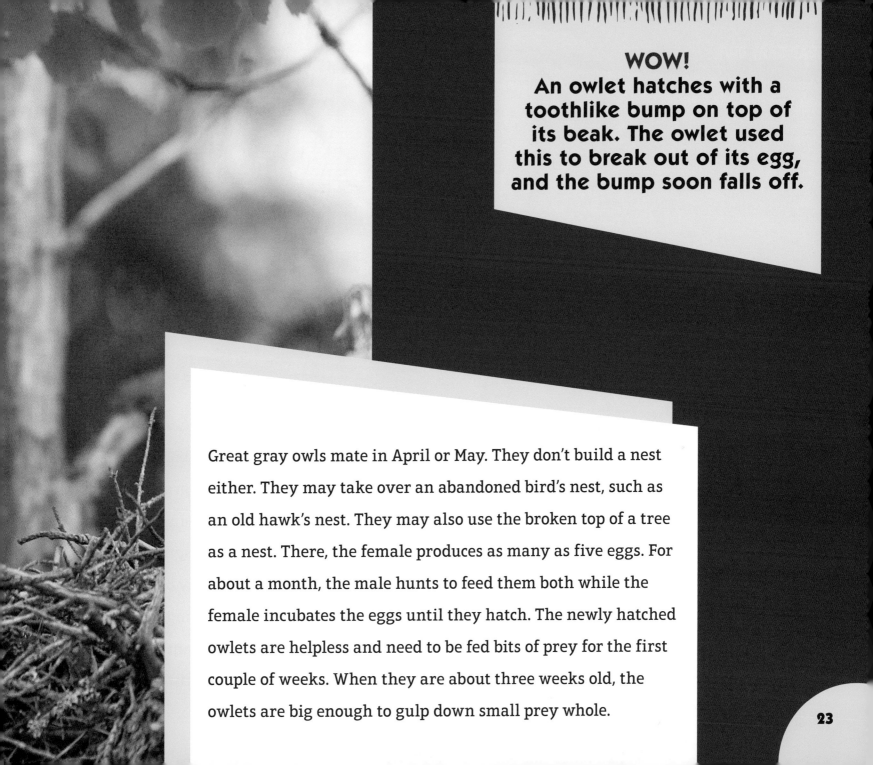

WOW!
An owlet hatches with a toothlike bump on top of its beak. The owlet used this to break out of its egg, and the bump soon falls off.

Great gray owls mate in April or May. They don't build a nest either. They may take over an abandoned bird's nest, such as an old hawk's nest. They may also use the broken top of a tree as a nest. There, the female produces as many as five eggs. For about a month, the male hunts to feed them both while the female incubates the eggs until they hatch. The newly hatched owlets are helpless and need to be fed bits of prey for the first couple of weeks. When they are about three weeks old, the owlets are big enough to gulp down small prey whole.

By the time the great gray owlets are about five weeks old, they've shed their baby down and grown adult feathers. But they still can't fly. So a young great gray walks along branches, flapping to strengthen its wings.

During this stage, a female great gray owl usually leaves the family and returns to hunting for herself. But the male stays and continues to hunt and drop food near the juveniles while they begin to fly and hunt for themselves.

When a Eurasian eagle owlet is about seven weeks old, it is nearly the size of an adult and getting its adult feathers. If both of its parents are away and a predator such as a fox or a lynx threatens it, the owlet tries to look too big and fierce to attack. It also clicks its beak while giving its fiercest stare.

EURASIAN EAGLE OWL

Once they're hunting for themselves, juvenile Eurasian eagle owls and juvenile great gray owls still stay in their parents' territories for three or four months. Then they head off to hunt for themselves. Both Eurasian eagle owls and great gray owls need two to three years on their own to become top predators where they live. Then they'll be ready to find a mate and raise another generation of top predators.

A NOTE FROM SANDRA MARKLE

Even top predators face challenges, and a global change in Earth's climate is challenging both Eurasian eagle owls and great gray owls in one big way. It's reshaping their ranges, the areas suited to their hunting and raising young. And climate change affects their prey populations. If their food supply shrinks, the owls raise fewer young to adulthood. Over time, that could cause a decline in Eurasian eagle owl or great gray owl populations, at least in some areas.

Most challenging of all is that as the climate warms, more people may move into the home ranges of these owls. As people clear the land and build homes, they can destroy the owls' habitat.

Photo by Skip Jeffery Photography

OWL SNAP FACTS

EURASIAN EAGLE OWL

ADULT SIZE
Females are up to 30 inches (75 cm) long with a 6-foot-2 (188 cm) wingspan and weigh up to 5.9 pounds (2.7 kg). Males are smaller.

DIET
They mainly eat mice and hares, but they may catch prey as large as foxes and deer fawns.

LIFE SPAN
In the wild, they may live as long as twenty years.

YOUNG
Chicks develop inside eggs incubated by the female for about a month before hatching. The female usually lays two to four eggs.

RANGE
They live in woodlands, grasslands, deserts, and mountainous areas of Europe, Asia, and northern Africa.

FUN FACT
What look like ears on a Eurasian eagle owl's head are just feathers.

GREAT GRAY OWL

ADULT SIZE
Females are up to 33 inches (84 cm) long with a 5-foot (152 cm) wingspan and weigh up to 2.8 pounds (1.3 kg). Males are smaller.

DIET
They mainly eat small animals such as mice and voles but may catch and eat rabbits.

LIFE SPAN
In the wild, they may live as long as thirteen years.

YOUNG
Chicks develop inside eggs incubated by the female for about a month before hatching. The female usually lays two to five eggs.

RANGE
They live in forested areas of North America, Scandinavia, Russia, Siberia, and Mongolia.

FUN FACT
When hot, a great gray owl pants and droops its wings to expose an unfeathered spot under each wing.

GLOSSARY

BEAK: an owl's hard, sharp-tipped jaws

DOWN: the fine feathers that are an owlet's first coat

EGG: the hard-shelled structure within which a baby owl develops

OWLET: a baby owl

PELLET: a compacted ball of the hard waste bits from digestion, such as some bones or hair, that the owl brings up. Then it lowers its head and opens its beak wide to let this pellet drop out of its mouth.

PREDATOR: an animal that hunts other animals

PREENING: the process by which an owl pulls feathers through its beak to fasten separated feather strands

PREY: an animal that a predator catches to eat

TALONS: an owl's claws

INDEX

Image credits: Andrew Kandel/Alamy Stock Photo, p. 3 (left); Carol Gray/Alamy Stock Photo, p. 3 (right); Ondrej Prosicky/Alamy Stock Photo, p. 4; Fredi Devas/Getty Images, p. 7; Rolf Kopfle/Alamy Stock Photo, p. 8; BIOSPHOTO/Alamy Stock Photo, p. 10; agefotostock/Alamy Stock Photo, p. 11; James de Bounevialle/Alamy Stock Photo, p. 12; All Canada Photos/Alamy Stock Photo, p. 13; Fran Walding/Alamy Stock Photo, p. 14; Arterra Picture Library/Alamy Stock Photo, pp. 15, 19; Daniel Hernanz Ramos/Getty Images, p. 16 (top); Jim Cumming/Alamy Stock Photo, p. 16 (bottom); o0oRichard/Getty Images, p. 21; imageBROKER/Alamy Stock Photo, p. 22; Donald A Higgs/Getty Images, p. 24; Arterra/Universal Images Group/Getty Images, p. 25; Edward Lee/EyeEm/Getty Images, p. 26; David Sainsbury/500px/Getty Images, p. 27.

Cover: Joe McDonald/Getty Images.

THE AUTHOR WOULD LIKE TO THANK DR. DAVID F. BRINKER AT PROJECT OWLNET, MARYLAND DEPARTMENT OF NATURAL RESOURCES, AND DR. DENVER HOLT, OWL RESEARCH INSTITUTE, CHARLO, MONTANA, FOR SHARING THEIR ENTHUSIASM AND EXPERTISE. A SPECIAL THANK-YOU TO SKIP JEFFERY FOR HIS LOVING SUPPORT DURING THE CREATIVE PROCESS.

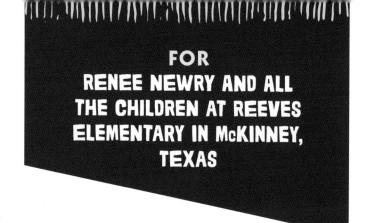

FOR
RENEE NEWRY AND ALL
THE CHILDREN AT REEVES
ELEMENTARY IN McKINNEY,
TEXAS

Lerner Publications Company
An imprint of Lerner Publishing Group, Inc.
241 First Avenue North
Minneapolis, MN 55401 USA

For reading levels and more information, look up this title at www.lernerbooks.com.

Main body text set in Aptifer Slab LT Pro medium.
Typeface provided by Linotype AG.

Editor: Brianna Kaiser **Designer:** Mary Ross
Lerner team: Martha Kranes

Library of Congress Cataloging-in-Publication Data

Names: Markle, Sandra, author.
Title: On the hunt with owls / Sandra Markle.
Description: Minneapolis, MN : Lerner Publications, [2023] | Series: Ultimate predators | Includes index. | Audience: Ages 8–12 | Audience: Grades 4–6 | Summary: "Owls are one of the world's top predators. These stealthy hunters can fly nearly silently, see long distances, and easily hear prey. Discover the hunting behaviors of owls and see how they train their owlets"— Provided by publisher.
Identifiers: LCCN 2021051332 (print) | LCCN 2021051333 (ebook) | ISBN 9781728456256 (library binding) | ISBN 9781728464428 (paperback) | ISBN 9781728462455 (ebook)
Subjects: LCSH: Owls—Juvenile literature. | Predatory animals—Juvenile literature.
Classification: LCC QL696.S83 M369 2023 (print) | LCC QL696.S83 (ebook) | DDC 598.9/7—dc23/eng/20211021

LC record available at https://lccn.loc.gov/2021051332
LC ebook record available at https://lccn.loc.gov/2021051333

Manufactured in the United States of America
1-50695-50114-2/10/2022